Help! I'm Talking to Myself

Help! I'm Talking to Myself

50 Speeches to Give Yourself to Keep from Going Crazy

Kelsey M. Maynor

 For information about this title or to order other books and/or electronic media, contact the publisher: Maynor Made LLC Decatur, Georgia 30034

ISBN-13:
978-1090855701

ISBN-10:
1090855702

Printed in the United States of America

Cover Design by: Creatively Olivia
Interior design by: Maynor Made, LLC

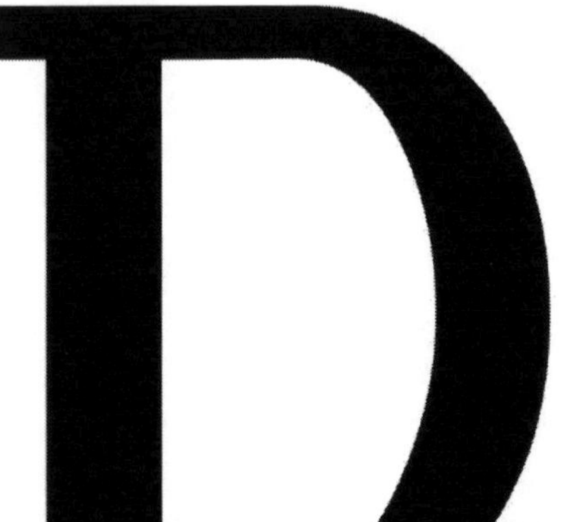

Preface

Preface

Life is a Rollercoaster. The ups and downs, loop the loops, twists and turns… they are just part of the ride. But what do you do when the rollercoaster gets to the top of the climb? The spot where it feels like you can see the entire city, and you raise your arms in the air and just scream, anticipating the *real* part of the ride: The DROP!

You get this sense of weightlessness… Whether you enjoy rollercoasters or despise them, once you get on, you are on it until the ride stops. If we can embrace every jerk, shake, and unexpected flip that comes with it, why not learn to enjoy the similar ride of our life?

I originally wrote this book as daily pep talks to keep me from sinking into a state of depression and sulking in self-doubt. I was afraid of how life started slinging me around and I forgot how to enjoy MY rollercoaster. My family and friends were unaware, but I was going through the Drop point of my life.

I was Homeless. I was sleeping in my car, on friend's couches, and at the gym. I was still managing two corporate shipping centers and traveling throughout the southeast on a speaking tour. I remember the nights leaning back in my driver's seat, hoodie pulled over my head, trying to sleep in the parking lot unseen.

This ride is for everyone. The climb may be different, the loops may be bigger (or smaller), and the drop can be critical, but we ALL experience it. I began talking to myself, and I eventually wrote the words down because I knew it would not be the last time I would need to hear these words.

These speeches and ideas stem from conversations I've had with close friends, family, mentors, and people I didn't know at all.

I dedicate this book to the people who have encouraged me, motivated me, housed me, fed me, listened to my dreams, helped me set goals, and reminded me that ALL THINGS work together for the Good.

I thank you, from every lub-dub of my heart.

Table of Contents

Table of Contents

Introduction

'Just Me and the Mirror'

What is your purpose? Your purpose is all encompassing. It's whatever has been revealed to you, whatever you dream about. Anything you work for! Your purpose can be a goal you push yourself towards, something you long to do, you feel the best doing, and anything you envision yourself doing in your future. Whatever you stay up late for, and wake up early, anxious to do. THAT thing right there, that is your PURPOSE.

In realizing your purpose, you may find yourself getting more and more frustrated as you envision doing what it is God has seemingly called you to do.
WHY?

Why? The reason is simple. You have BIG plans, BIG goals, and thus your purpose feels overwhelming. Not only is it overwhelming at times, it is confusing. When you talk to people about your purpose, there are two, maybe three, types of people you encounter.

- The "Hey that sounds great! I'm trying to be just like you" person.
  - The Inspired
- The "Yeah, more power to you, I see a lot of people doing that, couldn't be me, though" person.
  - Back Hand Complemented
- The "Another one? Sounds interesting, but how are you going to make money?" person.
  - The Realist or what I like to consider "The Mom"

However, the conversation goes, it leaves you wondering and questioning your purpose. You start wondering how practical it is or isn't.

Say it with me:
MY PURPOSE IS NOT PRACTICAL.

Your purpose is not practical. God has blessed you with the ability to not only see what He is going to do in your life, but He has given you an outline of what to do. Sure, it may seem vague, like looking at instructions from IKEA for building a bookcase, but hey, you can still see that it is going to be amazing! And that amazing you see pushes you to finish.

You speak with people and they look at you crazy. You talk to yourself in the mirror, and even your reflection looks at you like, "Wait a minute, WHAT?!?!"

Not only that, as you ponder over your purpose, you start asking questions like:

WHAT'S TAKING SO LONG???
WHEN WILL THIS POP OFF???
WHERE'S THE MONEY???

Repeat after me:
MY PURPOSE IS NOT PROMPT.

I know people have told you this before, but repetition is key, Rome wasn't built in a day.

We want overnight success. We want to feel that immediate gratification that comes with transitioning from aimlessly wandering in life to a living a purpose-driven life. Yet, we forget one thing, EVERY TIME. When you merge on the highway, you always start from the slow lane!

WHEN YOU MERGE ON THE HIGHWAY, YOU ALWAYS START FROM THE SLOW LANE!

There is a process that is occurring, so please do not rush it. Allow this time to groom you, remove from you the mess you have allowed to build up around you, and just enjoy the scrub down God is giving you. This is no quick rinse. You are getting THE WORKS. Exterior and interior cleaning!

Finally, we find ourselves trying to anticipate our obstacles. We anticipate our blessings; we measure obscure happenings, looking for patterns. You are really trying to pretend as if you have been here before, seen this before, and have the capacity to determine the future. You play too much. Cut it!

Let's hear it: MY PURPOSE IS NOT PREDICTABLE.

Your purpose has been engineered, strategically developed, laid down and illuminated to you bit by bit. You have never experienced this before; your mind cannot process the unknown. You simply live in La La Land until the blessings start raining in from the work that you are putting in. There is no expectation other than IT'S GOING TO BE AMAZING in a minute.

You just keep pushing.

You waste your time talking about the what ifs with the people who probably won't be there to remind you of the struggles – the sacrifices, studying, sleepless nights, skipped meals, missed outings, two-a-day workouts, 12-16-hour work days, should I continue? – when you were building… Yourself. You are going into an amazing space of the unknown and the obstacles you will face will be unknown.

Do not give up, do not turn back around, do not sit down, and do not get comfortable. Sure, you get frustrated and your mind wanders. Sure, it's not as easy as your simple mind expected it to be.

So, remember to stay patient because your purpose is:

- ☐ NOT Practical
- ☐ NOT Prompt
- ☐ NOT Predictable

But it will lead to an amazing, purpose-driven, goal-shattering, family-developing, community-changing, world-witnessing, life of abundance that is filled with fruitfulness and joy.

There is a purpose for your patience; you just don't know it yet.

1 You Better Get Ready

'You Better Get Ready'

Your blessing is right over the hill.

Today is not the day to take a lackadaisical approach. You must push yourself to the top. No one is going to do it for you.

Your Blessing: Your Work.

It's time for you to plant your feet firmly into the ground and get your hands dirty. Focus your mind intently on what needs to be done. Create a realistic to-do list. List five objectives that must be fulfilled today and get them done. Don't add anything to your list, and don't push anything off until tomorrow. Today is the day of work.

Your greatness depends on it.

Oh yeah, before I forget... Once you get ready to receive your blessing at the top of the hill, every obstacle you can imagine will be there like a wall; a fortress; a moat; a fire-breathing dragon; lions and tigers and bears... Oh My!

Yes! The last UMPH will be a big one.

You need to be ready to take on the world to get to your blessing. Don't you dare shy away now! You asked for, prayed for, begged for and pleaded for greatness. Now go work for it. Have faith, courage and belief that the obstacles that you will witness today are no match for your strength mentally, physically, or spiritually. It's going to be hard. It's going to be scary. It's going to be difficult, but you are harder and scarier, and you make difficult look easy!

You need to attack today like you have been training for this moment your whole life.

You got this!!!

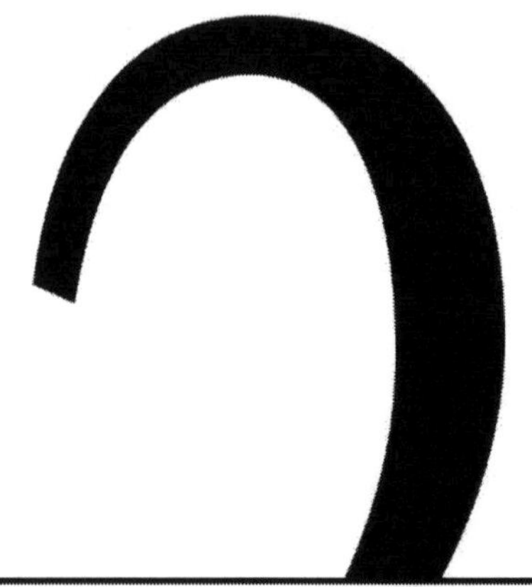

Who Are You?

'Who Are You?'

Who am I? I AM...

I am (insert your name here). I am human. I am a believer in life, hope, and the beauty of the natural. I am amazing. I am blessed. I am powerful. I am a force to be reckoned with. I am a gift from God. I am a follower of the Most High. I am a leader amongst men. I am a creation of life and a creator of life. I am an instrument used to promote positivity, love, happiness, and peace.

I am AMAZING!

I am obedient. I am rebellious. I am a voice worth hearing. I am a body for which you can lean on. I am a helping hand to lift you off the ground. I am a lighthouse to shine light on things that you may not see. I am a beautiful mind to bring knowledge to things, which you may not understand.

I am AMAZING! Did I say that already?

I am a beautiful masterpiece; designed, molded, carved, chiseled, sifted, and cleaned up for others to see, marvel at and emulate. I am a confident communicator. I am a confident lover. I am an eager beaver. I am a go-getter. I am a tenacious individual, ready and willing to go the extra mile for others.

Why? Because I pay it forward.

I am forward thinking. I am humble. I am respectful of my past, my elders, and those who came before me. I am thoughtful of the future. I am passionate about nouns: the people, places and things around me.

But most of all...
I am ME!

I am secure. I am a work in progress. I am a structure whose foundation is solid. I am rooted in my culture. I am diverse. I am wealthy. I am rich. I am strong and I am ALIVE!

Today, I need you to say these words. I need you to believe these words. I need you to live, (insert your name here). You are all of these things and more. I need you to know that today.

Who Are You?
Hmm... Let Me Tell You

Do You See What I See

'Do You See What I See?'

A great woman once said, "If you looked in my life and seen what I've seen..."

When you think about your experiences, the things you have seen with your own eyes, you begin to realize that these visual experiences have somewhat molded you.

Molded. That is a funny word. When I said it, I was thinking of molded as being formed, configured, gave shape to or influenced. However, molded also means spoiled, ruined, or tainted.

As we look over our own lives and truly examine some key experiences, we can determine if that situation really molded us or left us moldy from it.

Singer Mary J. Blige is known for her heart-felt, touching, dramatic, sorrow-filled lyrics of heartbreak, letdowns, and struggle. Her words have led many of us to connect, relate and understand her because we, too, have felt this way.

Life can be only what you make it.

In the song, "My Life", Mary J. sings, "Life can be only what you make it/When you're feelin' down/You should never fake it/Say what's on your mind/And you'll find in time/That all the negative energy/It would all cease."

Yes, Mary! She hits it right on the head. That's probably the reason why she appeals to us so much. This song speaks to our life experiences. Our experiences have given each of us a particular perception of the world we live in. Through our travels, our relationships, our upbringing, and my personal favorite, aimless wandering, we bring to the table this uniqueness in view.

My personal travels have shown me better and worse situations that I can then compare to my own circumstances, thus developing a broader and more macro-level understanding on my position in this world. Because we all do not see things the same, we need and must appreciate one another for the visuals of life that we have seen, and be eager to share our life travels with one another, both the ones that molded us, and the ones that left us moldy.

We must be eager to share our life travels with one another

As Mary J. closes out her song, she asserts, "And you'll be at peace with yourself/You won't really need no one else/Except for the man up above/Because He'll give you love."

She is right.

We have to find that peace within ourselves. We have to come to understand what it is we are seeing and what's happening to, in and around us. Most importantly, Mary J. has given us a way to take a moldy situation or experience and turn it into a molded opportunity where we are left built up rather than tossed out.

You must go out into the world and see some things, have some experiences and share them with others. Learning from both your moldy situations and the moldy situations of others will, in fact, mold you.

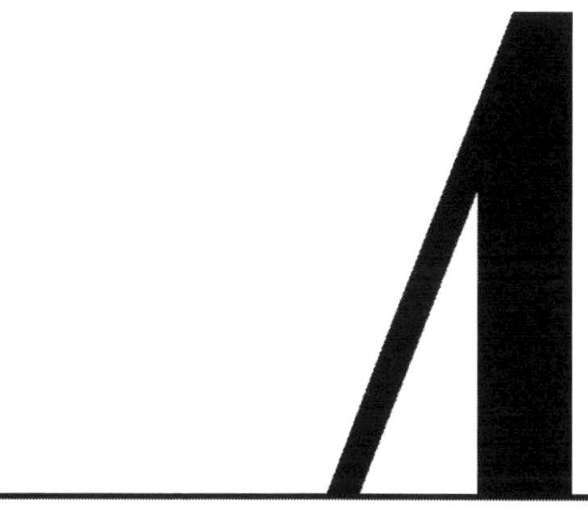

You Gotta Get Up

‘You Gotta Get Up’

You have been laying down long enough.

You have been in a transitional phase for some time, but I tell you that today marks the end of an era and the beginning of a new one. You have had trials and tribulations, victories and defeat. You have learned great lessons through your circumstances that will serve you well. You've been shaken by change, discouraged at the results of poor decisions, and many times have felt at a loss for direction. None of that matters anymore, though. You have got to stand up!

(Insert your name here), you can no longer saunter in sadness, walk in your woes, and lay in your lameness. What was, has, or used to be is just that. You need to see yourself successful. You need to see yourself confident. You need to see yourself happy. You need to see yourself being your powerful, beautiful, loving, kind, authoritative, brilliant, driven, joyful self.

Why?

Because... Seeing is believing.

It is time to leave the past behind. Step into a new day and achieve the greatness you see destined for yourself.

Nothing can stop you…

GET ALL THE WAY UP!

Everything is Everything

‘Everything is Everything’`

All you have is all you need.

You have to make some adjustments today, you need to realize what you have and truly understand what it is you need. You have enough to keep you happy, enough to make it in life; you have enough! **But why is it that you feel inadequate? Why do you feel behind in life? Who are you trying to catch up with?** Funny thing about perception, it becomes your reality.

I challenge you to search for the truth, understand the truth; matter fact, live your truth! Align your Truth with your Perception. Your struggle is your struggle, your challenges are your challenges, your triumph is yours, the victory is yours, and “the power is yours.” –Captain Planet

Align your Truth with your Perception.

Your struggle has called for a celebration because you have accomplished some great things in your life, but it does not feel like enough.

You feel behind, like others have gotten a head start. Your friend just posted on Instagram with a new luxury car, your cousin just got married, and let's not forget about that couple you follow that has been traveling the world this year. They make you so very happy, and yet completely disgusted at the same time. **What are you doing with your life?**

NOTHING!!!

Correction! You are living an amazing life. What you have accomplished is great thus far. You must start seeing your life as the truth it is, and then just be eager to add on to it.

Consider yourself blessed, because what you desire is luxury. Luxury comes after the necessities have been handled.

You have what you need to succeed.

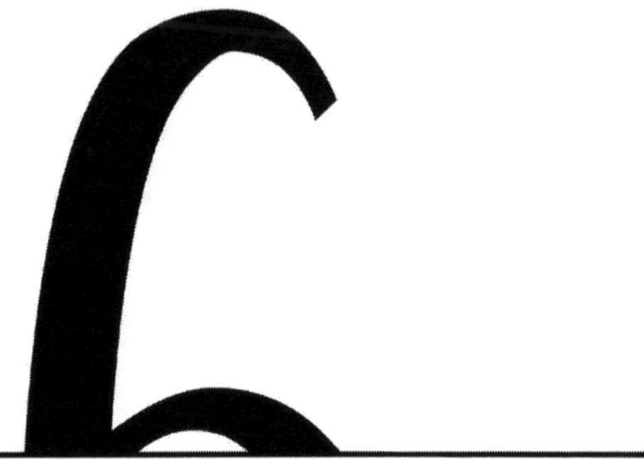

6 Help Me, Help Me Please

'Help Me, Help Me Please'

Needing help is not a weakness!

We have been predestined for Greatness, each and every one of us - but it doesn't stop there. We have been predestined for greatness and called for a purpose. Because we have been called for a purpose, our actions have been justified, and through our works, we will be glorified. However, there is a catch! The hardest part about our trek of life seems to be understanding the middle. That long haul of the onset of adulthood, where we have to start figuring things out for ourselves, is so difficult. It is a combination of not knowing what to do or how to do, and not wanting to ask for help.

So, let's break this down really quick:

We have the initial understanding of our greatness. We all know that from jump, or at least everyone acts as if they are the best things since sliced bread, Instagram, and Uber. Now here is the beginning of our troubles.

We have to understand our Calling for Greatness. We often get calls from everyone else. Every 'Hey Stranger,' Sallie Mae, Pay This Bill, 'You Have Won a...,' but we miss that greatness Call. You play phone tag with that it. But once you and your calling finally meet each other, your purpose is developed.

Is it just me, or does realizing your purpose feel like a breath of fresh air? When you jump out on faith for your purpose, that fresh air starts to smell stank. Like everything that could go wrong, does go wrong.

But more importantly, you understand that you start messing up. The people, places and things you start doing begin screwing with your greatness.

This is when you need HELP the most! This is when you start crying for help, kicking and screaming with frustration, having anxiety, and feeling like you are drowning.

- We have to be reminded of our strengths. Reminded of our own abilities. Reminded of our brilliance of our purpose, our love, and many more times, of our greatness! Many times, the greatest help we can receive is a reminder... You think you are drowning, but I tell you, you can swim. You think you are losing all your money, but I tell you, make one call can and will stop the leak. You think you're failing, but I tell you, your greatest success comes from what looks like a demise.

You have to REMIND yourself of the greatness within.

The Bible says something I want you to remember and take to heart, "those He predestined, He also called; those He called, He also justified; those He justified, He also glorified. And if God is for us, who can be against us?"

- Romans 8:30-31

Needing help is not a weakness, it is a strength.; a strength to overcome your pride, your own understanding, and a strength in those around you to be able to support you.

“I think I have to send you a reminder, here it is.”

- Jay-Z

7

Don't Wait On It

‘Don't Wait on It’

You won't get far, fast, hesitating.

The cloudy fog of the morning haze has drifted to the horizon, presenting to you this path-this stony walkway. This yellow brick road leads you into the direction of your greatness. On this day, a path has been revealed...

This path leads to your dreams and ideas that seemed so farfetched, so huge, and so unobtainable. It is showing itself in a way that you feel things can now be achieved.

Well for the most part you see the path. It doesn't quite connect to your dreams, but the steps are there. You can definitely see the steps leading you to your destiny. It is still kind of blurry though, and all the stones don't really line up for you to walk on. It is more like a skip, jump, hop, and a balancing act.

To be honest, I am not sure the path is a path, it kind of looks like random rocks on the ground.
Stop!

You have got to be kidding me!!!

You cannot sit around expecting your life to be written out for you like the plot of your favorite movie or television show.

Finally, every wish you have ever wished granted. Every prayer you have prayed answered, and all your wants and needs met... yeah, Yeah, *what's the catch?*

You have to walk! Going along this path, and it might not always be step-by-step or day-by-day. It very well could require some creativity on your part to run, jump, and leap in the process. But you are making progress!

It's no longer just a thought. You can see it happening, and you have a route to get there. Sure, you can't see all the way down the path, but the beginning is clearly right in front of you.

There are two things you need to do to obtain the greatness, which is yourself:

Step One: Walk!
Step Two: Repeat Step One!

I'm Not Ordinary Anymore

'I'm Not Ordinary Anymore'

You have to blossom where you are planted.

There is a story we all have heard regarding the comeback kid; he or she being the deprived, under-developed underdog that ultimately becomes strong, victorious and successful. However, we often miss the 'How' in these narratives.

How do these success stories begin their climb to greatness? What does the groundbreaking look like?

Let's first look into the gardening process. In order for a seed to be planted safely, the ground has to be broken, or tilled. The ground is chopped, disassembled and aerated, meaning the seed needs space made available in the soil for it to grow and breathe.

Second, a hole is dug, and the seed is placed below the surface.

Below the Surface!

Remember that.

Now, here is the beauty. This seed, planted in a hole, is covered by soil, and the expectation is for this seed to take root in the foundation, sprout, and grow above the soil. Let's make sense of this...

You have been looking at other's success stories and comparing them to your stories of failure. You are looking at the sprouting or the green glow of growth and said to yourself, "Wow, look at that. That is amazing!" You want that success, you want that greatness, but what you need to be saying is, "How did they make this so amazing?"

You cannot compare your unplanted seed to the sprouting of someone else's.

You have found yourself in a place of disruption where it appears as if your situation is experiencing an earthquake. Things are shaking up, but do you feel frightened? No! You know what it takes to become great.

In order for your seed of greatness to grow, you will find yourself in a place of confusion that will entail some tilling, shaking, and sifting. After that comes the planting in a hole. This is the test!

You have to blossom where you are planted. You have to see the place you are in as the bottom foundation from which your greatness has to grow. It is not pretty or glamorous in this dirty hole we call entrepreneurial life, but it is the most important part. Here is where your roots spread, latch on to core ideals and find out what it takes for you to survive.

The hole is important for you to grab hold of the fundamentals of you.

From here, you press your way through the soil, going against gravity, but luckily for you, the soil has been tilled so that you can grow quicker and easier with little debris.

When you sprout, all that you have been through, all your frustration, anxiousness and excitement, will explode into a dance of pure joy.

Each seed is unique in what it becomes once it makes it to the top, but the process is systematic. It will always start in this manner. It is God's recipe for greatness.

Let's Sprout!

Do You Understand?

'Do You Understand?'

Free up some space for that passion to take root!

You were created to make a difference, to change, to develop, to push forward, to break down barriers, and most importantly to grow. Yet, we have found ourselves in this place where everything seems to just interest us but nothing really takes root.

Do you understand what that means?

You have many interests, many things you could do, but nothing seems to stick, nothing seems to truly touch your heart and nothing ignites in you a strong desire to pursue it full on. I am curious as to WHY. Let's examine what it takes for something to take root and grow...

There are insecurity walls you have put up that must come down.

The most important part of the entire planting, growing, farming, and development process is the soil, the foundation.

Is your soil ready to be planted on? What does that even look like?

Well in order for soil to be prepared, it has to be tilled, broken up, loosened, fertilized, and debris, such as rocks, removed.

Write your name, you have to break some things down in your life. There are insecurity walls you have put up that must come down. You have some old bad habits that do not allow you to succeed in this world. You have been through some COMPLETE BULL****, just as fertilizer, however you have not learned or grown from your past experiences as to utilize it for the nutrients or lessons it provides.

Write your name, remove those people, places and things that are stuck in, on, or around you that do not allow for your freedom. I am talking about those confining things, the naysayers, the negative vibes, the I'm just here for the benefits' job, the same ol' same foolishness... You have to free up some space for that passion to take root.

You have to prepare yourself for your next big thing. You have to do the prep work.

It Starts with You

10

Close Your Eyes

'Close Your Eyes'

Blind faith is easier when you don't think.

Think back to when you were a child and you were lying in the bed. It is pitch black in your bedroom, and your night-light is flickering in a very spooky way. You look at the only consistent light you can find, straight out the window lies the moonlight barely grazing your windowsill. Suddenly, you start seeing figures moving. You can't make heads or tails of things, and now the strange noises begin. You hear creaks, thumps, thuds, bangs, bumps, and everything just seems to get louder and closer to your dark room.

AHHH!!! Is there something in my room???

You throw the covers over your head and squeeze your eyes shut.

It's funny how when we get scared, whether watching a scary movie, walking through a haunted house, or even becoming overwhelmed by a crowd, we close our eyes. Oddly, closing your eyes in sight of danger does not make you any safer, nor does it make you suddenly invisible to the threat or fright ahead. Yet, we often close our eyes when these situations arise.

We find this sense of safety behind our closed eyes, our hand-covered faces, and even under the warmth and thickness of our comforters. Ironically, comforters for beds do just that, comfort.

It's the faith we have in this moment of blindness that is intriguing. I'm speaking to those who have faltered. You began well. What hindered you? You believed the lies of the enemy and allowed them to undermine your faith in the plan and purpose for your life. You have become weary in the battle and have allowed yourself to become weak. Stir up your faith again and do not allow anything to interrupt your flow. Close your eyes and see yourself through. I need you to envision your success, your safety, your comfort, your wildest dreams coming true, and come to peace with yourself.

Refuse to sit down, give up, or go back.

Today, close your eyes, but not in fear. Close your eyes in comfort that your moment of blindness creates a sense of trust, peace, and ease.

Blind Faith.

Finish It Off

‘Finish It Off’

Today needs to be the day you overcome the obstacles. Today needs to be the day you jump over the hurdles of life. Today is the day you outrun the haters nipping at your heels, and you throw your voice as far as you can see.

You ought to be swinging with all your might. Today is the day that you are going to have to fight for what you say you want. If this is, in fact, your purpose, your passion, your desire, your love, your dream, TODAY is the day to prove it.

Don't get stuck in “can't”.

You are going to have to do more than just say it. You are going to have to do less when you do it. You have to show it. And not just show it, but prove it!

Unfortunately, this is not going to be easy, but it is doable. It is achievable! You are capable! You are amazing! You are strong! You is beautiful! You is kind! You is whatever you need to hear to keep you from quitting, to keep you from giving up, to keep you keeping on!

YOU HAVE TO GO FOR IT!!!! ALL THE WAY!!! RELENTLESSLY!!!

Today is the day of MOTIVATION, DEDICATION, and last but definitely not least, CELEBRATION!!

There is just one thing we have to do to make this possible.

See that thing you started? It is right there after the N... CAN'T. You see it?

Look closely. You started to draw that line but you stopped! Let's finish it today!

CAN'T

CAN|T

CAN

(Insert your name here), you CAN do this!!!

12 It Is Time

'It Is Time'

This is what you have been waiting for! The time has come for you to step up. Whatever hesitation you have been experiencing needs to go away.

Be reminded that "NO" is an anointed word, and you don't have to apologize for using it as often as is necessary. The enemy will accuse you of being heartless and will send a hefty dose of guilt and condemnation your way, but this attack is a seduction. It is designed to lure you into countering a haughty spirit with haughtiness and control with a power struggle when "no" is sufficient.

I am sure you are thinking, "THANK YOU!" So now you are planning to just say no to every person who asks you for a favor, for every event you have been invited to, etc. However, I am speaking more to you. You need to have the self-reflection to tell yourself no.

Just Say No!

NO! You do not need to go out tonight and spend any money. NO! You do not need to buy those new shoes. NO! You do not need that Biggie Size Coke. NO! You do not need smoke when you wake up. NO! You do not need extra salt on your fries. It doesn't have to be a fight, just stand your ground and maintain good boundaries. Begin to separate yourself from those things that are not benefiting you.

It is time to do right by you!

13

Relax

'Relax'

Do not get worked up about so much.

Things are always going to be there that just tick you off. Those mishaps, miscommunications, and just plain stupid situations you find yourself in will NEVER go away.

We are talking simple things like a flat tire, ripped jeans, or a coffee spill on your shirt. We're talking about that time the iron left a wet brown stain on your white shirt, or you dropped mustard from your lunch sandwich, stepped in dog poop as you cut across the grass heading to a meeting you were late to, or the worst, traffic in the middle of the day. I mean the time your phone died in your hand on 15%, or when you reach into your pocket and realize you left your wallet at home. I'm talking about the time when you were riding in an Uber and the driver gets lost.

Do you understand that things just happen?

You are waiting at the barbershop/salon even though you made an appointment. You and your friends are out to eat and you do not like the meal or the price you paid for it...

We are going to practice one thing, one thing we are going to consistently do until it becomes a habit. This one thing must be a part of our everyday lives. It is a true character adjustment.

This one thing is *CHILL.*

You have to be able to find your peace. Relax your mind and don't panic, overreact, or hold on to the funk that life often tries to sit right in your lap.

You have got to learn how to relax. Your body, hair, hair edges, kids, teammates, spouse, and the world will all thank you if you learn to just CHILL.

CHILL OUT!

14

Truth Behind Hope

'Truth Behind Hope'

HOPE: to want something to happen or be true and think that it could happen or be true.
But what is it that you hope for?

We hope for the new house, new car, new position at work, an increase in income, decrease in stress, more time to enjoy life and all our things, and we definitely hope for a loyal, trusting, and fun spouse.

Then two questions arise: How does this hope make you feel, and what's the reason behind the hope you have?

Hope should make you feel empowered!

You should have hope for the future that your future will be bright, exciting, vibrant, and prosperous. Your hope should wake you up at night and have you jotting down ideas to apply to your day. Your hope should have you mentally examining options, developing yourself and bettering situations. Your hope should be contagious, so much so that you kind of want to infect people with it.

However, you need to be prepared to tell everyone the reason behind your hope. What is your hope based off of?

This is when you have to tell the TRUTH! This is your backing to why the heck you believe in what you believe in. You have to tell about those days when ramen noodles, George Foreman grilled chicken and canned veggies were your life, and how you prayed for the vision and all the hell you went through. Smile when you say it.

I have set goals, hoped to achieve them, and then surpassed them.

Why?

Because you can say, "I WAS there, but NOW I am here. I've BEEN through some mess, and I hoped to get out, and I DID! I have set goals, hoped to achieve them, and then surpassed them. Not just once, but time and time and time and time and time and time and time... AGAIN!"

The reason you believe in the HOPE is because of the TRUTH you already have experienced in your situation.

Here is one very simplistic visual of hope and truth. My son is riding in the truck with me, and the gaslight comes on with a BING! He looks at me and says, "Daddy, we have to get some gas! We are gonna run out and get stuck on the side of the road." (Obviously, he has been through this struggle before.) I tell him very calmly, "I hope we make it to the gas station." I am calm. Not only am I calm, but CONFIDENT in the TRUTH that we WILL make it to the gas station. I know from experience that I have roughly 15 more miles left before my car is out of gas, and we are stranded ---
SO...

Hope is backed by the truth that I KNOW!

15

Do It

'Do It'

It can't be THAT easy, can it?

A man came to me the other day and said that he has been trying to get his life in order. (Shoot, you and me both!) He is a professional sports player, and success came to him before manhood did. Through the many words he spoke, he ended by saying, "I just want to do what God is telling me to do, man. Can it be that easy?" It made me think of the following story…

In Luke 5, Jesus is walking and teaching on the shore of the lake. He asks Simon to take him in a boat just a ways off the shore to speak to everyone and get their attention. Simon agrees, and it is there that Jesus continues his teaching, just far enough out that everyone could see and hear him.

After he finished, Jesus asks Simon, who had just cleaned his fishing nets for the day, to go back out to the deep part of the water from where he had just come. Simon states he had been out there already, all night even, and that he had caught nothing.

NOTHING!

Simon said, "Okay. You got it, Jesus," and there he caught more fish than his boat could handle. There were so many fish that his net began to break, and he had to signal to James and John to come over with another boat to help. Their boat overflowed with fish, as well.

This, I tell you, is a simple metaphor. Jesus took an ordinary fisherman, tired from a long night of doing what he does; Fish! Simon was not the pillar of his community. He was not the priest or minister of the town. He wasn't even an upstanding Christian. Simon said, "Go away from me, Lord; I am a sinful man!"

We want something, need something, pray for something, but we DO nothing.

There was one thing Simon did, though. This one thing was so simple that we often miss it. We want something, we need it, we pray to God for it, but we DO nothing. Simon, against his own judgment and expertise, just did what Jesus asked him to do.

Now back to you…

You have asked God for a blessing before, and you were blessed to get that job and the many opportunities that came along with it. God is telling you once more, GO and DO. So be obedient and trust the Lord, because like Simon, his obedience got him more fish than he could handle. Simon not only received an abundance of fish for himself, but his blessing overflowed to other people, James and John, who were able to come along in the moment.

Look, you are outgrowing your place.

Follow the Lord, be obedient, and see how your blessings will not only overwhelm you, but also overwhelm those around you. "Don't be afraid," Jesus said. "Come with me."

The last part of this story gets overlooked all the time. We tend to forget that when things start moving in our own lives, there are people watching us. Jesus has a crowd on the shore watching him as all of this action takes place on the lake. The amazement Simon experiences ran over to James and John, who are a part of the blessing. Those on the shore are not only astonished, but they are motivated, inspired, and encouraged by the acts they are witnessing.

Don't Be Afraid...

JUST DO IT

16 It Will Be a Good Day

'It Will Be a Good Day'

This is going to be a powerful week!

Why? Because I said so. Start speaking it.

Have you ever spoke something into existence? Of course, you have.

You told yourself there were no good men or no good women in your city! And guess what, you haven't found a good one yet. You said you hated your job, and it was a waste of your God given abilities. Guess what? Yep, you're still wasting your talent.

Have you ever spoke something into existence? Of course, you have.

You watched the news last night and said," Man, minorities can't win." Oddly enough, you are absolutely right. So, since you are batting 1000, why not swing for the fence?

Declare that today, tomorrow, this week, this month is and will be powerful, amazing, life changing, and it will be the best of many more!

This is your chance to use your power to speak the best into your life.

If you woke up this morning, God has given you the breath-to-breathe life into something and someone. Stop biting your tongue and holding your breath. Let out the song of praise that's cooped inside of you. I need to hear it, and the person at the desk next to you may need to hear it, too. The old woman in the grocery store line in front of you may need to hear it. Your best friend may have woken up in the state of low, but if you are where I am, I'm looking at the clouds! All I'm saying is your excitement, joy, and love is contagious, and someone may need to catch the hype that you have! Give it up, because you will wake up one day in the Low; cold, alone, and you would NEED someone to bring that fire into your life and warm that spirit.

Stop being selfish!

17

The Pressure is On

'The Pressure is On'

Do you feel under pressure?

You are not alone. We all have felt the pressure, the weight, and the confinement of societal ideals defining who we are, what we do, and how we should do things.

When you are born, rules, boundaries and restraints mean nothing to you. You sleep when you are tired, you cried when you wanted to, and you move as your body allows.

We are immediately taken advantage of because we are seen as impressionable.

But!
As children, we are filled with questions, doubts, regulations, dos and don'ts, and How Tos. Notice I did not say "We Are Full," but that "We Are Filled" with questions and doubts.

Our individuality, our uniqueness and our gifts of greatness are harnessed. Now for some, harnessing your gift means to get control of or to gather in order to make use of; however, when you truly think about it...
Are you really harnessing your gift, or is someone harnessing you?
Your gift of greatness is hard to describe. It's not the job you

have or your dream career. Sad to say, but your gift of greatness probably isn't the child you have either. The difficulty we have in understanding our gift of greatness is we have been conditioned to make things black and white.

Things are either this or that.

Think of it this way. You are really interested in visuals. You like creating displays, putting things together to help people understand using props. Oh! Oh! You are a lover of music, music of almost all genres, and you even take pictures. Really good pictures! The World then harnesses these interests and streamlines you into what lane, what box, what arena?

Marketing! Yep, you guessed it.

"You will be perfect for marketing." So that is what you begin to pursue, marketing. However, you are not fulfilled. You do enjoy the visual aspects of marketing, but marketing as a whole does not fit you.

Hmm... So, where does that leave you?

You are correct! BRANDING!!!

You live for Branding. You take your creativity and put it with visuals, and concepts and music and video and everything is great! Until it isn't…

You have been under pressure to pursue a career based on set ideals. If there are four lanes on the highway of success, the world tells you pick A lane and ride it out.
Well I am telling you, to change lanes, move about freely. Heck, take the street, take a helicopter, or a plane. Get there

how you feel like getting there.
Why?

Because there is one thing I know oh so very well:
If everyone is streamlined mentally to get on the highway of success and to stay in their respective lanes, there will be Traffic. And there is no reason to be stuck in traffic.

There is a reason why we celebrate people when they find their individuality.
Don't get it twisted! It's not, how do my goals align with my career? Instead it's, how does my career align with my life goals?

I need you to do ONE thing... Figure Yours Out!

18

Does this Look Familiar

'Does This Look Familiar?'

Have you been reliving similar situations, over and over and over again?

In grade school, teachers would create habits through repetition. If there was a word, sentence, phrase or lesson to be learned, a teacher would have you write it down. However, just writing it down once was not nearly good enough.

Vocabulary words were instructed to be written several times for homework. If you found yourself in trouble, you would be instructed to write your lesson on the board repeatedly until it was ingrained in your memory. Homework assignments often included several questions centered on the same concept.

There is a lesson to learn in repetition.

We seem to miss it. You have been working this job for a few years now and you are ready to quit, just like the last one. Maybe you are in a relationship, and it has gotten to a very similar UH OH moment as the previous. You are ready to let it go, too. What about that time last year when you vowed to change your eating habits, and here you are, writing up a grocery list to lose weight, AGAIN! We are seeing a pattern in our lives, a consistent revolving of similar feelings, situations, and problems.

The question then becomes, are you going to keep circulating, or are you going to break this cycle?

Sit back and find the lesson in this and then make the necessary adjustment. Maybe these repeated scenarios are for you to try again and make the right decision this time. Maybe you haven't learned the lesson yet, so the situation is recurring until you recognize it, and can shout 'DEJA VU' and know what to do.

Don't Get Stuck in Insanity.

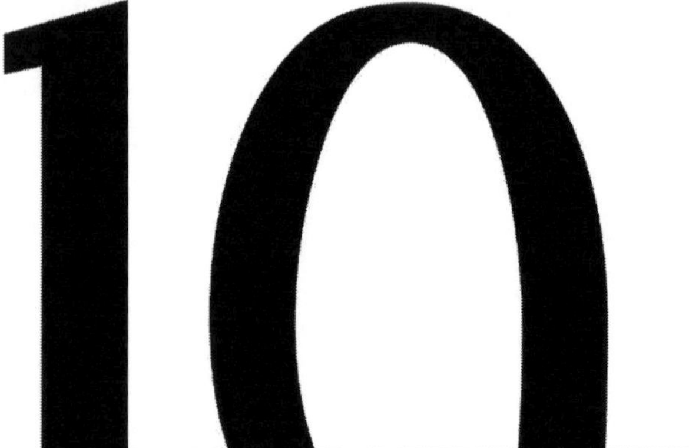

No, No, No

'No, No, No'

It is okay to say no. It really is.

Saying no can be so liberating. It is like a sense of relief, a weight off your shoulders, and it can even be an exhilarating experience. Having the ability just to say yes or no is a blessing in itself.

Choices! You have the power to choose.

As you make this trip to find your peace, passion and purpose, you begin to hone in on what best works with you, for you, and by you. I recommend you doing this one thing: write down your own personal mission and vision statement. Just as you would for your business, declare what you stand for and believe in, what you intend to accomplish and even who wish to influence. Once you have written this down, remain focused on it. Whatever does not align with your mission and vision statement, you can feel at ease when you denounce it.

I believe the best feeling I have ever experienced in saying no is turning down a job offer. Yeah, it sounded good. Sure, the pay was okay, but it did not align with where I was heading. Maybe finding your purpose and aligning your work is not the problem. Let's make it basic.

You are the person who always, always, always goes on a diet before the beach trip, before summer hits, right before it gets cold outside, then again before the class reunion. Oh, and let's not forget that diet you do when you get out of whack spiritually. Yeah, that fast with no prayer thing. You find yourself constantly going on diets rather than just living in accordance with your personal health goals, mission and vision.

> Say no to those snacks you pick up at the grocery store.
> Say no to the invite to go out for late night dessert.
> Say no to that job if you are intending to have a career.
> Say no to that boss who treats you like crap, but when you threaten to leave, they offer you something.
> Say No! Say No! Just say… No!

You have to start making choices that lead to your victory!

It's Almost Over

'It's Almost Over'

Your Second Wind is Coming!

Take a deep breath and regain yourself. Do not panic; that only makes things worse. You may feel like you are drowning. The 'To Do' list may seem to keep growing, and that pile of work your boss dropped on your desk today may look insurmountable. But maybe that's not you.

Maybe your issue is that the vision of your success and the tasks required to achieve this success are just all out of whack. You are walking a path, yet each step you take is in the dark. You have no clue how to get there, and your phone is saying 'NO SERVICE.' FML! You are wading in the water, doggy paddling for what is starting to feel like forever. You are TIRED... but not for long.

You have to keep your head up.

This phase will pass. You have to keep your head up, and for goodness sake, stop screaming for help. If you think too much about how hard it seems right now, you will feel like you are dying, for real. Remain stayed on the prize; LIVING!

Living to you may be blowing your boss away with how you completed all that work before the deadline and to perfection. Or maybe living to you is proudly stating your business has picked up traction and is basically a self-operating machine. Freedom... now THAT is living.

So, get free from seeing your right now as your forever. There is this crazy thing that happens when you get that small taste of success, when you see that peak of light at the end of the tunnel, when you can see the finish line. You just start going for it harder. You kick it up a notch. You just want to finish so bad that all the pain goes away, and nothing but pure, shredded passion pushes you.

You better not QUIT when you are this close to Living! Just Keep Swimming!

21

It's Not Easy to Win

'It's Not Easy To Win'

And there is only one way I know how to make a life easier… get through the crazy stuff so that the hard stuff won't faze you.

It's something like this:

As a kid, you played; I mean you played hard! You fell, got back up, scraped knees, bumped your head, knocked out a tooth, broke an arm, fractured a finger... BUT you are here to talk about it WITH A LAUGH!

You used to be scared of monsters under your bed and in your closet. You fell headfirst to the ground after hanging from the monkey bars. You got your heart broken when you and your family moved from your hometown. You were destroyed and depressed when your parents separated. You were devastated when your grandparents, the ones you spent so many summers staying with, died. You were beaten up in high school. Beaten by love. You have been let go, fired, and/or quit a job; a job you needed to pay your bills. You have played HARD! For many, these mishaps, these bumps, these failed situations mean you have a ROUGH life. However, making your own path requires you to explore areas uncharted, to cut down trees,

Making your own path requires you to explore areas uncharted.

shrubs and grassy areas that are blocking your way; to dig up mess that is deep-rooted and latched on to you. You have to force your way through to make New. Life is easier because you have been through difficult things, SO much so that small issues, medium issues, and other hardships shouldn't faze you.

I call it being “rooted in chaos”. It creates a sense of calm in you. Why? Because you’ve seen the monsters under your bed. You have been with the skeletons in the closet. You've seen death, destruction, failing communities, and the broke life. Because of that, life is not scary to you. You now know how to overcome it. No sweat!

The hard doesn't feel so hard anymore. What gets others nervous, uncomfortable and flustered does not bother you. WHY?

It is because you went from thinking you could not make it through difficult times, to experiencing difficult times, to actually making it through difficult times.

Thus, you no longer **hope** you make it, you **know** you make it!

Stop Beating Yourself Up

'Stop Beating Yourself Up'

(Insert your name here), you have got to stop it!

Self-doubt will get you nowhere fast. Yeah, I am sure you have made a mess of things before. I'm sure you probably single-handedly sabotaged every relationship you have been in. If you are anything like me, you have gotten to the second- or third-year mark at your job, and you somehow lose it. While everyone else seems to get comfortable in their cushy jobs, getting engaged or married, their kids look smart and happy, the house looks nice -- shoot they have a house, here you are, still renting, leasing a car, single and failing to mingle, hating the job you seem forced to work, still in school wondering, "Oh Lord, what is I gone do?"

You are going to stop cheating yourself.

All the mess-ups, all the failures, and all the dead ends you have experienced don't make you DAMAGED.

YOU ARE NOT DAMAGED!

You have to see the good that comes from the experience. You have been through some things; eyes been opened a little wider.

Your feelings have been hurt, you have some skin in the game, but most importantly, You Are Here, meaning that you have not been taken down. <u>HOW?</u>

I don't know how you do it. I would have given up a long time ago, but for some odd reason, you keep getting back up. You keep on coming back. You can't be stopped. You are like a roach, goodness!

Why doesn't that impress you? Why doesn't that motivate you? Why are you not entertained? You have been through all this mess and you're still here to talk about it.

(Insert your name here), don't you get it...

You <u>are</u> Unstoppable!

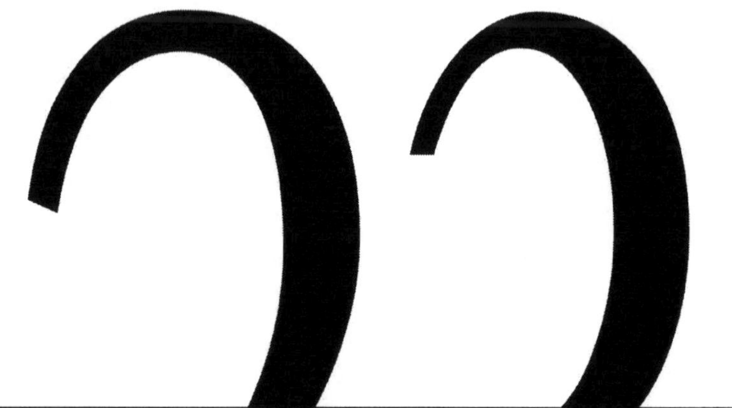

Yell on the Inside

'Yell on the Inside'

Drive on the Outside! You have this burning desire inside of you. This passion that rumbles in your spirit, it's hard to explain to people, hard to put into words, and hard to reveal to others. You just can't seem to get it out. Frustration builds up because you long to express this desire, but when you try, it just comes out like gibberish. Many ideas just spew out of your mouth.

There is this idea and that idea, this plan and that plan. Oh, don't forget about this part and that part, and then the non-profit you want to start. And as that person stands there seemingly wiping off all the mess you hurled on them, they are at a loss. Loss of understanding... Here's how this should go...

> I know you have dreams, visions, passions, desires, wants, needs, plans and ideas. Shoot, We all do!

Internally, I know you have dreams, visions, passions, desires, wants, needs, plans and ideas. We all do... BUT, how do they tie into one another? Do they tie into one another? No, I'm not saying limit yourself to one thing, or that you can't be great at multiple things. However, what I am saying is that there is ONE HUGE thing that you are going to do with your life that encompasses all of those other dreams, visions and aspirations.

Think of it as one big show with multiple seasons and many episodes. Figure out what that BIG thing is that you want to do. All those pieces of you will then be laid out to you like a stairway. This part will lead to the next and so on. You won't always be able to convey all your dreams and aspirations, and that frustration will drive you...

Put it this way:
It's hard for me to explain...
Let me just show you.

Makes Me Wanna Shout

'Makes Me Wanna Shout'

Sometimes you have to shout it! Hey (insert your name here), I'm feeling something today... Are you with me? Today ought to be the day that you just give out a shout of praise. You have been working hard all month. The goals you set for yourself, you have achieved. The obstacles that stood in your way, you have overcome. The mess that almost, I said ALMOST, got you stuck in your old ways, you were able to speak your way through. Oh, I KNOW somebody feels me on this!

"Hey, stranger" texts...

I'm talking about those "Hey, stranger" texts from the old boo; the man/woman that came at you sideways, upside down and backwards wrong; the coworker who called you out in an email while CCing all your superiors; the car that swerved in your lane and just missed you. Maybe it was that night out at the bar when that person got so close to you that you almost forgot the pact you made with yourself to stay focused on yourself... *Hello? Are you still there?* Those "Ooh, YOU LUCKY I KNOW JESUS" moments that kept you from ALMOST losing sanctity.

You should be on Cloud 9!

I don't care if it is only the beginning and that you still have another twelve goals set for tomorrow, and the day after, and the day after. The excitement starts now. The praise starts now. You need to have MOMENTUM when going towards your destiny.

Think of praise like this:
You are running the 4x4 relay track race. The gun sounds, and your teammate takes off running. They are coming down the straight, they hit the curve tight, and they are getting closer to your handoff of the baton...

DO YOU STAND THERE AND WAIT FOR THEM TO RUN TO YOU?

My question to you is:
Are you going to let your teammate sprint all the way to you, while you are at a standstill???
NO!
As you see your teammate running towards you, you put your hand back, and you start running towards your goal. The teammate yells, "Stick," which means I am handing the baton to you. Your teammate is in mid stride, you are in mid stride, and there is no loss of momentum. You take the baton and you run with all your might!

So let's try this. Instead of just praying, you try a little praise with it. Shout out a good praise to get the juices flowing, so when that blessing hits your hand, you are already going.

Take a lap, and see if God doesn't bless you with a mile!

Ain't Worried About Nothing

'Ain't Worried 'Bout Nothing'

You can't worry about all that mess! (Insert your name here), you have to focus on what NEEDS to be done! You have been given a vision, passion and purpose, and your steps have been ordered, so …

What exactly are you worried about?

We spend too much time, money, and effort doing things for the wrong reasons. That new outfit, suit, or shoes is not going to help you close that business deal.

You ordering a filet mignon at the conference dinner is not going to impress anyone. Sure, people tell you that business deals are made on the golf course, but honestly and truly, if that were the case, why do we even have offices?

The more extra mess you pick up along your way, the more you have to worry about.

You have to remain stayed on your path. The more extra stuff you pick up along the way, the more you have to worry and keep up with. You get that? The more extra mess you pick up along your way, the more you have to worry about the extra stuff you picked up...and you can't worry about that mess!

If you were to ask any real successful person about their plight, you will hear these three things.

They focused on what God told them to do. (Something about their religion and remaining governed.)

They made a lot of mistakes.

Half the mess they worried about or did was a waste.

Successful people will often tell you that once they made it to the top, half the mess they thought was important, what they thought would matter, what they thought meant something actually MEANT NOTHING.

So, I say to you today,
Don't Worry... Be Happy

Do You Have Authority

'Do You Have Authority?'

If you don't buy it, you can't sell it!

Let's talk about what you like to talk about. Making money! It's crazy, but it's true. Whatever you are selling, you must first buy. I'm talking about everything; your personal brand, clothing, ideas, beliefs, products. Whatever it is, you have to buy into the idea first. You have to be your first fan, first subscriber, first test dummy - the guinea pig, the client.

You have to experience it!

Once you have experienced it, and you still believe what it is you are putting out, then NOW WE ARE GETTING SOMEWHERE.

Understand this idea called authority.

There is a process to authority, and in order to have an authority, these things must happen:

Understand It: Let's say it is your business concept, new teaching method, study strategy, or working process. You have to believe it works in your mind.

Experience It: You have to know whatever it is you are talking actually works. Consider this the testing period. Is the idea dope? Does the process lead to better results? Does it decrease wasted time?

Do It: Once you start doing it, you will have a more focused and direct method. You will have a goal, and you know the outcome you are looking for is obtainable. Why, because you have already done it before.

THIS IS WHERE AUTHORITY COMES INTO PLAY!

You have the authority in your voice because you believe in what you talk about. But not only that, you know it works! So, when you speak, there's a passion and an understanding! Together. Aligned.

In the Bible, Mark 1 tells of Jesus being baptized by John the Baptist, going forty days in the wilderness while being tempted by Satan. While in the wilderness, he remained focused and steadfast on what he understood of the Word.

Jesus exits the wilderness, recruits four disciples, and does his first teaching in a synagogue. The people in the synagogue stated they had NEVER, EVER heard someone teach with such authority. WHY?

Because Jesus understood the Word, experienced the Word in action while in the wilderness, and did what the Word said to do. He SPOKE what he KNEW to be TRUE! HE SPOKE WITH AUTHORITY!

Repeat after me: I've Been There, Done That, and Won That… Already!

Behind the Scenes

'Behind the Scenes'

You aren't just an actor? We are enthralled by the elevated camera shots, seemingly crashing down from the sky. The trees are zooming past us, birds are dodging, and sunrays lunge towards us at every break in the tree leaves. We plateau behind the legs of someone walking. The street seems busy with pedestrians, and then the walking stops. The camera rises to the shoulders of a man standing at the street's corner where we see the back of his head. He turns around abruptly, as if we are encroaching on his space. He yells directly in to our face, "HEY!!!!! That's my wallet! Thief!" The camera shot darts right. The shot is jumpy, dashing past blurred streetwalkers, cars, and spins right into the side of a patrolman.

-Scene-

Film and videos are merely retellings of life experiences.

The film and video industry is the best example to understand the thwarted importance of in front of and behind the scenes. The many hands, minds and bodies that go into scene creation will blow your mind. This one scene we just read requires cameramen, lighting experts, audio technicians, extras, a traffic controller, wardrobe, craft services, and the list goes on. Here's the connection...

Film and videos are merely retellings of life experiences. Your everyday life has so many moving parts, so many pieces, and there is so much effort that goes on behind your scenes. This world was created with you in mind. Your movement, interactions, and environment are seemingly a staged production; and as an actor in this production, remember this: you didn't make the scene. You are just a participant in the process.

There are people doing things when you are not aware; praying for you when you aren't even praying for yourself. Saving money to help you when you don't even know you need it, speaking your name as to introduce you in the future; putting down a trail so that you can walk it tomorrow. Breaking down barriers so that you are not confined; and building bridges so you can cross large obstacles with ease. Somebody is working for your good!

The question then becomes, are you working for theirs?

Tell somebody today:
Oh, We Working Today!

Stand Up for Yourself

'Stand Up for Yourself'

You have to speak up. There is little time for hesitation, for silence, and little time for someone to stand in your place.

Why are you hesitating?

Often, we lack confidence in our decisions. We feel as though we need time to digest, time to examine, time to figure out where our minds and hearts lie on the situation. You are stalling; stalling because you aren't prepared, because you aren't sure what you know in your mind, stalling because you don't know your heart enough. You are stalling because your heart and your mind are rarely in formation, rather they both wander, aimlessly, individually...

You are stalling.
Stop!

You don't know in your mind and you have shaky feeling in your heart. You either make no decisions, or you make decisions that are one-sided. Both are bad. Your mind suffocates the action because your decisions are overly thought-out. You can't allow things to be, or you make overly emotional decisions where your heart is overzealous. Whether in happiness and excitement or hurt, agony and frustration. Either way, you need to stand up for yourself, unified! Mind, body, and spirit.

HOW? How am I going to get my ish together?

Be Prepared: If you read more, stay abreast on current events, past events, philosophies, technologies, ideologies, etc. You need to be learned. Most importantly, you need to prepare yourself for yourself. Know yourself better. Self-reflect, journal and examine you. Find your morals, your beliefs, and foundation.

Have Faith: Your faith is measured by your belief in what you know and feel. Faith is what you know in your mind and believe in your heart. You will make better decisions if you have faith. Why? Because there will be no reason to hesitate. You were prepared for this already, now make the decisions.

Follow Through: Just because you have it now doesn't mean you will keep it. The hard part isn't making the decisions all the time. The hard part is often continuing to make the decision, keeping your word, and completing the task, every time.

Are you standing in your own way?

Plant Your Seed

'Plant Your Seed'

Have you ever planted something; a seed, a flower, a word? What's the first step? Digging a hole. You have to dig a hole to plant a seed. You could, however, just throw your seeds over the ground, but you risk having your seed washed away by the rain.

You have to churn up the ground, till the soil, break up some things in the ground, shake up some dirt, and make a place for your seed to be planted. The ground can't be even, it can't be flat. It has to be disturbed, broken, chopped up. There needs to be some holes.

There needs to be holes first before a seed can be planted.

When we go out into the world, why is it that we so often ignore those who have dug themselves into a hole physically, mentally, emotional, and spiritually? People around us are hurt, broken, chopped up.

The world has chewed up and spit them back out, and we walk right past them every day. The people you talk to don't want to hear you, and the people who need to hear you, you don't want to talk to.

We are expected to plant a seed, reap a harvest, share our testimonies, build up our neighbors, grow our communities, raise our children, but we insist on doing that where the ground is level, settled, flat, or already developed. If we understand the basics of growing something, we should be planting on tilled land, where it is already prepared. People are waiting on you to plant a seed, a seed of hope, of inspiration, motivation, and encouragement: a conversation.

We must go where we are needed.

Go For It

'Go for It...'

As soon as you stop worrying. We hold on to what is comfortable, convenient, and easy, yet we complain about it being stifling, boring, or a waste of our gifts. Now is the time to step out on faith. Now is the time to take a chance on you. You have committed forty hours a week, five days maybe six, endless phone calls and meetings, conference calls, and trainings... FOR WHAT?!

What have you learned?
What have you retained?
What can you do with it?

It's time to execute all that you have been bragging about! Be the hardest worker, the most creative, the best networker, the greatest note taker. Be the sales rep, the customer service agent, be your job title. But be it for yourself. Don't check out of work when you clock out. Still be that person to yourself.

Don't be afraid to go jump! It's not that far of a fall if you have been constantly developing your wings...

How will you know until you try?

31

Forgive and Forget

‘Forgive and Forget’

For Give! For Get! For Give! For Get!

Understand this: If you do not forgive, you will not forget. It is a simple concept once you look at the wording. You are expected to give and you expect to Get. Well, in order for you to get, you have to give. Does the phrase “give and take” sound better for you?

Those grudges, hostage feelings, bickering and quarreling, hate, dislike, frustration and anger you hold towards people in your present and your past will remain in your future.

Don't give me that blanket "I forgive you"

Imagine yourself walking down the street. You see a homeless person on your path, and you see them panhandling (begging). Once it is seemingly your turn in line to be approached, you immediately start patting your pockets and shaking your head as to say, "No, I don't have anything for you." Why, because you've given money before and witnessed it being used for drugs or whatever. Now...

Your anticipation and preparation to say NO is like you asking the bank for a business loan. Sure, you may have a compelling story and a solid business plan, but the banker has seen your kind far too many times and has probably been burned by the likes of you. So, NO is the predetermined answer to any of your inquiries.

Is this FAIR? Heck No!

For Give, For Get.

The Lesson: You must be ready to give what is given. You must forgive to be forgiven. You have to be ready to give a blessing if you expect to get a blessing.

FOR GIVE, FOR GET. GIVE, GET.

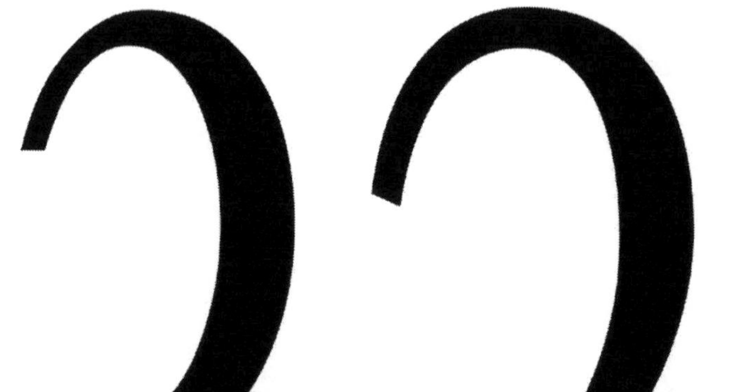

So What's Your Function

'So, What's Your Function?'

Oh, you just want to be cute? It's overwhelming at times, this thing called life. We take great pride in beauty. We are attracted to the looks of things, to brightness of colors, to the twinkle of gems, to shapes and feels... to the point that we idolize those things we consider beautiful. Idolize! It has surpassed the point that we appreciate function. Function has no use. The aesthetic, however, there lies our sight.

See, these things look good, but something isn't right.

- Eyebrows on done… but you've got bad skin.
- Wealth, but bad health.
- Dope haircut, bad teeth.
- Good looks, but stay at your momma house?
- Tall, but can't play basketball.

Can one tell the difference between a caterpillar, which turns into a butterfly, and one that becomes a moth? Probably not, yet the butterfly is the one we call beautiful. The one we wish upon, the one we admire, the one we stare at with joyful grins. However, the butterfly is truly a WEAK creature. They fly slowly, and they are nimble and delicate in nature. The moth, however, is stronger, faster, and more agile, and yet we choose to see it as ugly. Don't get stuck being so cute that you don't function. You have a tremendous purpose on this Earth. Be strong, quick, agile, and cunning, AND who said you can't look good doing it? Be the best of both worlds.

33

All That I Can Say

'All That I Can Say'

You Better Talk That Talk! You have to go into the room with the mirror that allows you to look right into yourself. That mirror you stand in front of to see if your hair looks good, if your outfit came together like you wanted. That mirror you look into before you have to go speak to some important people. That mirror that shows you yourself. That mirror that makes you talk to yourself.

GO FIND IT!

Whether you are standing in front of yourself, one person, or one million, you must speak with authority. You must speak with your heart. You must speak with love, and you must speak with the intentions of life. The power of the tongue is SO powerful, and I don't want you talking death into yourself anymore.

The power of the tongue is SO powerful.

When you look in that mirror, you see a fighter and a contender; a victor! You will be victorious! The words you speak to yourself go to your heart, so stop giving yourself heartache. You are stronger than that.

You have greater control.

TAKE CONTROL!

What you say, how you say, why you say will affect your day. So, on today, speak joy in it, declare it great, and proclaim yourself victorious over opposition. You better talk that talk and walk that walk, and remember many times you start that walk by yourself. Talk to yourself, comfort yourself, build yourself, and love yourself...

SPEAK IT

How to Love

'How to Love'

We don't know what to do with ourselves.

It's wild how we operate sometimes. We think we know everything. We think we have learned it all. With love, we have been there, gotten burned, and thus we know about love. But we don't know about love, we know about deceit, heartache, pain, and frustration. What we should know is what to do with ourselves after we have a messed-up relationship.

We don't know about love. We know about deceit, heartache, pain, and frustration.

If you love someone with your heart, that's a feeling. Feelings come and go, but your mind has to also align. You can't love someone and still THINK you are no good. You can't love someone and THINK it's ok to go through his or her phone! WHY? Because that's not love thoughts. Thoughts of deceit, infidelity or curiosity have taken over.

I don't care what your last relationship looked like, you have to LOVE in your mind and LOVE in your heart, TOGETHER, AT THE SAME TIME. Both have to align. You can't love the thought of loving someone and not be passionate about the pursuit and constant building of love for, in and around someone.

The heart and mind are disconnected, but we need them both to operate together in order to LOVE. It must penetrate our hearts and be written in our minds. We have to feel love and see it written... But thirdly, we must speak it.

1. See Love
2. Feel Love
3. Speak Love

It's one thing to see it for yourself, another thing to feel it, but when you speak it, you share it, you confirm it, and you declare it. So, if you are 1 out of 3 or 2 out of 3, YOUR Relationship fails under pressure, adversity, and scrutiny. We have to hold these three ideals about love together.

I KNOW MY LOVE, I AM PASSIONATE ABOUT MY LOVE, AND I SPEAK MY LOVE!

Do You Have It?!?!

'Do You Have It?!?!'

It's complicated, I know. We have to understand how this thing works. It's a little complicated. Just like when you play a sport, you have to understand how the game is played. You have to know the rules! There are plays, different moves, strategies and objectives, but knowing the rules is not enough.

Your coach would yell, "Play with some heart!" But how, when you have only learned how the game works mentally? How am I supposed to play with heart? Where do you get this heart?

Your mind and your heart operate separately of one another. Your brain has no control over the heart. You can't make it beat; you can't make it stop, you can't make it go faster by thinking faster, and you can't necessarily make it go slower with your mind. It seemingly acts by itself. If you were to lose your brain function, your heart still goes on lub-dubbing. BUT…if your heart stops, you stop!

What's a game of heart??

The heart operates off love. Love for the game, love for the sport, love for one another, a love for life. So even though you understand mentally how the game is played, you will gain nothing playing without heart. You may understand your spouse and how they do things, but your relationship, marriage, family will gain nothing without hearts filled with love. You have to understand the mind and the heart.

It takes two baby...
MIND & HEART

I'm Hungry!!!

'I'm HUNGRY!!!'

I have tasted success, and I am craving it. Every day you walk the streets, you go to work, you meet people and you hold conversations. But lately, your conversations have been different. You haven't been communicating the same way. You haven't been loooooong talking, listening to anyone gossip, or entertaining counterproductive banter. What has happened is you have gotten a taste of success, a taste of new, a taste of greatness, and now you want more, so you are operating differently. You are in search of something. If it doesn't look like greatness, smell like greatness, feel like greatness, you are gone, in search of greatness.

Sift out and find those people who are able to help fulfill this hunger for greatness.

It's getting to be that time where your hunger for success, greatness, and change is no longer satisfied with the meaningless portions, servings and cuisines that you are providing for yourself, or that are being provided to you. Do you understand? The FLUFF has got to GO! Just like when you realized that fried food and candy are counterproductive to your health, the same applies to your interactions and conversations. Not to say you shouldn't be open and willing to communicate, but you have to be able to accomplish something.

We aren't talking just to talk... what do you want?!

Our greatness often lies on the connection we make with other people. Sift out and find those people who are able to help fulfill this hunger for greatness. It's not a solo thing. I am great because you are great. Thus, we are great!

You can’t be great by yourself.

Come On Already!!!

'Come on Already!!!'

You have put in so much hard work, sweat equity, yet you don't see the fruits of your labor. Sure, people may tell you that you are doing a good job, that they are proud of you, or the classic "I see you" statement. Yeah, it feels good to hear people sing your praises a little bit, but those words fall on deaf ears when you aren't able to see the impact of these alleged great works.

Where is my Six Pack?!
Where are those graduating high school students I mentored?
Why hasn't my credit score jumped yet?
Why haven't I gotten a raise?
Where is my BREAKTHROUGH?!

What we have to understand is this key lesson: A tree planted today will shade tomorrow.

A tree planted today will shade tomorrow.

Sometimes the planting of seeds, watering of the plants, and the blossoming or harvesting of our plants happen in other lifetimes. Your hard work and effort may never produce in your timespan, which is far different from saying it will never produce. Just as the tree planted today will need watering, pruning and sunlight, so do the seeds you planted in your life. You may influence a child today, and the fruit of that seed planted may not manifest until that 9-year-old has reached college ten years later. Your credit score may not jump immediately, but your diligence will prove beneficial when your first house is purchased.

We have to remove immediate gratification from our list of expectations because our influence may be written internally as an etching of hope, encouragement, motivation, strength, and love right there in the heart of someone. These etchings remain imbedded, never seen by our eyes.

Where is my breakthrough? Right beneath your nose...

Get Rich Quick

'Get Rich Quick'

Share the wealth. You are human, and as a human, money means more to you than your health sometimes. You will sacrifice your livelihood, your weekends, vacations, children, and families. Shoot, you will even sacrifice money for more money. You want to get rich quick! You want to have a million in your bank account yesterday!

What if I told you the secret to getting rich quick was actually to share the wealth first? You have an entrepreneurial spirit. You want to start your own business at some point.

Share the wealth.

You want to break free from the 9-5, the Monday - Friday, or even the weekends you spend building someone else's dream. But is it because you want to be the boss? You want to have something to call your own? You would rather work your own business rather than someone else's? I, I, I, Me, Me, Me?

Your business WILL make you rich when you share it. Your business will create jobs, pay employees, grow your community, and it will better the world in some instance!

Here's the idea: Go out and find people who can assist in this business venture, say, five people. You as the visionary must empower the other four. That four, along with yourself, will go and find others down for the cause, motivated to build on to your vision. Let's say you find a hundred. That hundred is empowered enough to just speak on the brand you are establishing, just enough to entice ten thousand your way; say via social media. Are you following me? Share the wealth. It grows faster when others feel like they have a stake in it.

This is not YOUR BABY. This is YOUR BUSINESS!

It takes a village to raise a child, and it takes a community to grow a business. You want to get rich quick? Create something and let others run with it while you go create something else. REPEAT!

In the words of a complex compound thinker named Future:

Forty thou' to a hun'ed thou'
A hun'ed thou', another hun'ed thou'
Three hun'ed thou, five hun'ed thou
A million, let's have a money shower

LET'S GO DO THE MONEY DANCE!

It's Not What It Seems

'It's Not What It Seems'

Get off your high horse. You are great! You are talented! You are blessed! Your hard work and dedication need not to go unnoticed, nor do they need to be boasted. Make sure you remain determined to do the work. Understand that just because you planted the seeds and watered the plants, it doesn't mean you made the plants grow!

We have all been blessed with some amazing talents, skills and abilities. Unique in our own way, success just seems to appear in all that we touch.

Of course, WE understand the hard work, dedication, loss of sleep, diligence and the effort that WE have put into our goals, but who else cares about all that?

Success just seems to appear...

Oh, you want some praise, huh?! Let's come to terms with this one:

> You reap what you sow, YES! Second line reads: The one who sows to please their *sinful nature will reap destruction.
>
> *Sinful nature = Selfish ambition, dissension, invoking envy, etc.

You are AMAZING at what you do, and so is God. So hey, I have an idea!!! Ya'll should work together, put him in your credits as the Producer, the Editor, the Writer, the Director… shoot, you know it's going to be dope, whatever it is.

Don't Be Settled

'Don't Be Settled'

We have all boasted in some way, shape or form that we refuse to settle. Typically, we are referring to our choice selection in mate/spouse/boyfriend/girlfriend. However, what we should be unsettled with is our current state of being. We should strive endlessly and passionately to live outside the box of confinement that we have placed around our minds. There is a box around your dreams, life, and success. Don't be settled in your box. There is so much more.

There is a box around your dreams.

This box restricts us from seeing far enough, experiencing more, and doing all that we can. We think we can't. Thus, we don't! We see the lines of failure and imagine ourselves tripping over them, and thus we experience a FEARFUL life. We operate within the confines of our mental cage.

We are cage-minded!!! BREAK FREE.

Challenge yourself to learn something new. Learn to play one song on the piano, rock out a jazz chord on a guitar, sew a pillow case for your couch, make a headboard for your room, write a short story about anything! Oftentimes, we want our hobbies to be linear with our professional goals and our business ideas to be relevant with our degrees, BUT sometimes you just have to...

DO SOMETHING DIFFERENT!

Lock It Up

'Lock It Up'

What are you going to do? There are situations that seem to be on repeat in your life. Déjà Vu is an understatement! You come to the same crossroad every time, and what do you do? HESITATE! Why?

We have seen how the wrong decisions have played out; we have experienced the repercussions of our wrongdoing. We have even coached others on how to avoid the mistakes we made. Yet, we are still hesitating at the crossroad where now our knowledge and wisdom have guided us. You have to make up in your mind what you are going to do.

WHAT ARE YOU GOING TO DO?

Oftentimes, we find ourselves conflicted between two ideals typically described as our good conscience and our evil one. Knowing the illustration, we can envision what, rather, who we should be adhering to: The Good Conscience. If we know the Good Conscience is true, then we MUST lock away the Evil Conscience. Remove that option, cross that choice out, deny that as even being an influence in our lives. MUTE that fool!

I know one thing for certain: if you continue to make decisions influenced by the Evil Conscience, you will find yourself in a heap of mess; confined, trapped, and miserable.

Lock it up or get Locked Up!

What Did I Do?

'What Did I Do?'

Being the bigger person blows. It's hard to be the bigger person. It's hard to do right when you feel wronged, to care when it seems no one else does. It's hard to keep going when everyone is through. It's hard to settle down and pray about it. It's hard to seek wisdom and knowledge when people are expecting you to act up and act out. It's hard when everyone is amplifying you to RE-Act!

It's hard to run when people say walk. It's hard to stop when people yell go. It's hard to be you when everyone is being someone else. It's hard when the rich dress poor, and the poor dress rich, and the woman isn't a Queen, she's more comfortable being a bitch.

We have to be leaders and stop this morality switch. We must lead. We must control our emotions and situations and take what we feel and truly give some concern for human life. It's hard work leading! Matter of fact, leading sucks.

Am I being punished with the gift of leadership?

You are called to be a leader! You can and will be the front of a great mission. Others will look to you for guidance, wisdom and knowledge, and you are expected to help guide and educate others. It's not a punishment; it's a blessing. You are the answer to someone's prayer!

GO BE THAT PERSON!

43

Isolation is a Beast

‘Isolation is a Beast.’

Animals of prey use strategic and tactical methods of isolation in order to attack and seize their target. Divide and conquer, if you will. The idea is that when one is separated from its group, support, and protection, then one is easier to capture, manipulate, and destroy.

Divide and conquer!

The idea works for many, but it should not work against you. You have been raised a certain way, you have read books, developed ideas, and have created a foundation solid beneath your feet. Those who have mentored you, instilled morals within you, supported you, encouraged you, and built up your confidence are your pillars of foundation.

You, my friend, cannot be separated from your foundation! You may feel like the enemy has isolated you, taking away your friends, family, etc., but you have and will always have the support created in your foundation. You will be able to stand tall on this structure!

Isolation is a beast.

Sure, it’s raining. Sure, it’s cold, and sure, you feel lonely. Isolation is a beast, but you have to understand that you are on an elevation. When you are by yourself, do not be afraid. You are a conqueror! The lessons and trials that you have overcome, you now stand on top of. You are not alone. You are elevated on the shoulders, backs and accomplishments of those who lift you up. Your foundation is your company, and you cannot be separated from it.

You cannot be conquered...
CONQUER DIVISION!

What is it That You Need

‘What is it that you need?’

We have to figure out what we are fighting for. What are your goals? What are your plans? What outcome are you working to obtain?

Do you know?

I am sure whatever it is, it's amazing, life-changing, world changing, and monumental even! Whatever you need to obtain that outcome, to reach your goals, and to fulfill your plan will come. It will come. It will be unique, and it will be based off what you need. But what the heck is it that you need?

Once you have an idea about what it is you need, try thinking about what that random person who just walked by you needs to reach their goals. Imagine how grand their ideas are. How big their goals may be. How much help they need reaching them, and how long or how short it will take them to get it.

> You need to focus on your goals, your aspirations, and what it is you need to get there.

You have no clue, huh?

EXACTLY.

What the person next to you needs will be different.

If it looks like they are getting a lot, they very well may need a lot to get their goal accomplished. What it is you need, you go and get that. Go make your enormous, amazingly prolific, life-changing, world changing vision a reality.

What you need, you will get, but what you do with it IS ON YOU!

Kicking and Screaming

‘Kicking and Screaming’

At some point, we have got to change. Stop fighting against your better judgment. You know what feels right, better yet, you know what IS right. Stop choosing wrong.

The way in which you make decisions leaves you drowning. What if you made the wrong decision? What if you picked too hastily? Was that the best option? Should you have waited for something else or someone else? What if you handled situations differently from start? Would you even have to make these decisions?

We drown ourselves in our doubt. Why? Because we lack faith; faith in ourselves, faith in our decisions, and faith in God.

> Faith. We ain't got it, but at some point, we have got to change.

Character building requires a lot more taking away and then adding on, at first. You must build yourself up in knowledge and wisdom. Then, and only then, will you not only feel more confident in your decisions, but your decisions will be backed by something. Whether this something be a past experience, a book learned comprehension, or a life lesson from observance, you will change as you challenge, expand, develop, and build your mind.

However, this requires you to admit you don't know, that you aren't wise, and that you make bad decisions. AND THEN CHANGE IS COMING!

Stop kicking and screaming, trying to remain the same.

STAND UP RIGHT.

You will change as you challenge, expand, develop, and build your mind.

Do More. Be More. Grow More.

46

It's Has Got to Go

'It's Has Got to Go'

Throw that mess away already! Listen, the way in which you walk is FREEDOM. You should smell like, look like, and speak like FREEDOM.

Freedom should be so evident that what you produce glows! It will shine, shine because you do. You have been set free to be great.

Your past mistakes, slipups, transgressions, sins, and blatant ignorance hold no place in your future. All that baggage, hurt and pain are self-inflicting and can be done away with, BUT you have to throw that mess away already.

All that baggage, hurt and pain are self-inflicting.

You can hold on to it no longer.

The longer you allow the trash of your past to fester in the now of your freedom, you will never experience freedom to the fullest. Matter of fact, you will find yourself seeing freedom, yet living in slavery.

Say it with me: I NEED TO LET IT GO!

Get Free, Stay Free

'Get Free, Stay Free'

Stop second-guessing your greatness. We must understand that we have been afforded and rewarded freedom. The only thing we have to do is remain free. Erase that mindset and those laws that you were forced to abide by. Stop second-guessing your greatness because society once deemed your expressions intolerable, unacceptable, or even unappreciated.

You want it? Go get it. Why? Because you are free to move about. You want to start that, start it. Why? Because you are free to move about.

Stop second-guessing your greatness because of society.

The very moment you second guess yourself and your freedom because of what society says or had said before, you will start sinking to the bottom of the lake; right after you were walking on water.

Have faith that you have the blessing, promise and truth regarding your freedom.

Now Go Be Free!

48

Find Your Joy

'Find Your Joy'

Who cares what people think? Celebrate your successes. Your happiness should be outright, in the forefront, and contagious. Every day, you must find the positive; that excitement in your life. Your small wins and accomplishments should inspire you.

Set goals, destroy those goals, set more goals.

Set goals, destroy those goals, set more goals, and then destroy those, too. Laugh at your trials and obstacles. Why? Because they have no clue what they are standing in the way of. Reflecting on your past and current wins, successes, and accomplishments will give you momentum, courage, and confidence. You will find yourself sitting amongst people with this grin on your face, a sparkle in your eye, a glow, a strong stance in your posture, and a power in your speech. Your joy will be noticed, and when you find yourself laughing to yourself about yourself, your future, and your success, don't be embarrassed. It's fine! Your success should make you happy.

Find Your Joy!

It Takes One to Know One

'It Takes One to Know One'

You will be as great as your vision is detailed. It's one thing to know what you are interested in, what your purpose is, and what the vision for your life looks like. But…You must be able to describe it, break it down, make it plain, see some of the ins and outs, and let your imagination run wild.

Take a look in the mirror and really visualize your success overwhelming you. Stare!

Look yourself in the eyes and let your mind develop your vision.

You begin to smile as the vision of yourself manifests right before your eyes. Do not shy away from this amazing person!

Rid yourself of habits that harp on your right now faults and blemishes. Learn to look in the mirror and see your future self, your "I've been working hard to get here" self.

When you begin to understand and truly know your purpose, you start to see similarities in others. Great minds think alike. Winners see other winners. Success makes amazing company. Influence finds influence.

You will see the greatness around you more.

Put a Little Umph in it

'Put a Little UMPH in it'

First, let's start by getting this out of the way: Whatever it is you want to do, you will fail.
Just know that your body will fail you.

It will trick you. It will try to make you stop way before you have truly even gotten to your halfway mark! At about 40% exertion, your body will say, "That's good enough." And because we tend to listen to our bodies, we, in fact, will stop! We will stop! And thus, when we stop, we f a i l !

The more you put out, the more you have to put in to yourself.

As your goals get bigger, your dreams become more vivid, and your passion burns stronger, you will have to grow with it. You will have to physically, mentally, and spiritually feed yourself more as you exert more. The more you put out, the more you have to put in to yourself.

You have to FUEL UP THAT UMPH!

So, the next time you feel like giving up, when your body is tapping out on you, and your mind is wandering, dig in deep and hold on because that UMPH is coming next, and you are about to go on a ride.

TAKE OFF, TAKE FLIGHT, and SOAR TO YOUR DESTINY!

Made in the USA
San Bernardino, CA
16 February 2020